Campbell's

CREATIVE COOKING WITH SOUP

Cooking with Soup... Your Way

Did you ever wish someone would write a cookbook just for you? Someone has, and it's different from any other cookbook you've ever used. That's because it's planned for flexibility—to help you with your busy schedule, your family's tastes, your budget, your food supplies, even your creativity.

Each recipe includes a unique chart that shows you how to vary ingredients to suit your needs. For example, if a recipe suggests peas and you don't like peas, you can use another alternative—possibly corn or spinach. If you're all out of cream of mushroom soup, the recipe might suggest using cream of celery. Or, if your budget favors tuna over shrimp, you can take that option.

Today's Americans are becoming more and more interested in the quality and nutrition of the foods they eat. They are learning that good food habits are essential to health and a general feeling of well-being. We at Campbell are excited about this trend. We believe that good food contributes greatly to the quality of life.

One of the easiest ways to balance your diet is to eat a wide variety of foods. Each single food has something important to contribute to your health, but it takes a combination of foods to complete the nutritional balance.

That's how this book fits into your plan for good eating. With the wide choice of ingredients in each recipe chart, you can easily vary your diet according to your nutritional needs and tastes.

These variations make every recipe a springboard to as many as 256 different dishes, for a total of more than 8,000 combinations in the book. The secret to making these recipes so versatile is the magic of canned soup. Cream-style soups start a foolproof sauce for dishes that require one; broth-based soups add a blend of seasonings to foods cooked with liquid.

If you're a beginning cook, you'll appreciate the simplicity of recipes made with soup. If you're more experienced, you'll enjoy the versatility of using soup to create your own new recipes.

You're already familiar with soup as a good old-fashioned food, but soup is also very contemporary. It goes into pasta and pizza, quiche and kabobs, tacos and stir-frys, even vegetarian main dishes. Besides these tempting entrées are fresh salads, full-flavored appetizers, hearty soups, even delicious desserts.

You can use these recipes with confidence because they have been carefully tested in Campbell's kitchens. Each variation has been created to work well with every other ingredient combination on the chart. Once you start using the recipes, you'll find your own favorites and you'll see how well they fit into your busy lifestyle. Yes, this book really is written for you!

How to Use This Book

Each recipe in this book consists of three parts: an ingredient list, a chart and preparation instructions.

Souper Easy Quiche

Ingredient List

4 eggs
1 can (10¾ to 11 ounces) condensed **Soup**
½ cup light cream
1 cup shredded **Cheese**
Meat
½ cup **Vegetable**
1 9-inch unbaked piecrust
Ground nutmeg

Chart

Soup	Cheese	Meat	Vegetable
Cheddar cheese	sharp Cheddar	½ cup diced cooked ham	drained, cooked chopped broccoli
cream of mushroom	American	6 slices bacon, cooked, drained and crumbled	drained, cooked cut asparagus
cream of onion	Monterey Jack	½ cup diced cooked chicken	sliced mushrooms
cream of celery	Swiss	½ cup diced cooked turkey	drained, cooked chopped spinach

Preparation Instructions

1. In medium bowl, beat eggs until foamy. Gradually add **Soup** and cream, mixing well.

2. Sprinkle **Cheese, Meat** and **Vegetable** evenly over piecrust. Pour soup mixture over all. Sprinkle with nutmeg.

3. Bake at 350°F. 50 minutes or until center is set. Let stand 10 minutes before serving. Makes 6 servings.

Simply read the ingredient list as you would a normal recipe. When you come to an ingredient in **bold** type, refer to the chart. Choose from one of the options listed below the heading. For example, for 1 can condensed **Soup**, look under the heading "**Soup**" and choose from Cheddar cheese soup, cream of mushroom, cream of onion and cream of celery.

There are 2 ways to use this chart. You may choose all the items from a single horizontal row as indicated in red or you may skip around as indicated in green. Once you have made all your selections, just follow the numbered steps.

That's all there is to it! You'll be preparing new recipes in no time.

Appetizers

✙

Appetizer Cheesecake

2 tablespoons butter or margarine
1 cup zwieback crumbs
1 can (10¾ to 11 ounces) condensed **Soup**
1 container (15 ounces) ricotta cheese
2 packages (8 ounces each) cream cheese, softened
Cheese
2 eggs
1 clove garlic, minced
Seasoning
1 cup sour cream
Topper

Soup	Cheese	Seasoning	Topper
cream of celery	1 cup grated Romano	¼ teaspoon thyme leaves, crushed	caviar and sieved hard-cooked egg yolk
Cheddar cheese	1½ cups shredded Cheddar	3 tablespoons chopped fresh chives	sliced cucumber, green onion and fresh dill sprigs
tomato	1½ cups shredded Swiss	½ teaspoon basil leaves, crushed	tomato roses and green onion tops
cream of chicken	1½ cups shredded Muenster	1 teaspoon curry powder	chutney

1. In small saucepan over medium heat, melt butter; stir in crumbs. Press mixture firmly onto bottom of 9-inch springform pan.

2. In food processor or large bowl, combine **Soup,** ricotta cheese and cream cheese. Process with food processor or beat with electric mixer until smooth. Add **Cheese,** eggs, garlic and **Seasoning.** Beat until smooth. Turn into prepared pan and place in jelly-roll pan.

3. Bake at 325°F. 1½ hours or until puffy and lightly browned. Cool completely in pan on wire rack. Cover; refrigerate until serving time, at least 2 hours.

4. Spread sour cream over cake; garnish with **Topper.** Makes 16 appetizer servings.

Cheese Ball

1 can (11¼ to 11½ ounces) condensed **Soup**
¼ cup salsa
3 cups shredded **Cheese**
Seasoning
Coating
Assorted crackers

Soup	Cheese	Seasoning	Coating
bean with bacon	sharp Cheddar	1 clove garlic, minced	chopped fresh parsley
chili beef	Monterey Jack	½ teaspoon hot pepper sauce	finely crushed corn chips
split pea with ham and bacon	American	½ teaspoon dry mustard	chopped walnuts

1. In medium bowl with mixer at low speed or in food processor, beat or process **Soup,** salsa, **Cheese** and **Seasoning** until as smooth as possible. Cover and chill 4 hours or overnight.

2. On waxed paper, place **Coating.** Shape cheese mixture into ball and roll in coating until well covered. Serve with crackers. Makes 1 ball, 16 appetizer servings.

Avocado Dip

1 can (10½ to 10¾ ounces) condensed **Soup**
1 package (8 ounces) cream cheese, softened
Seasoning 1
Seasoning 2
1 ripe avocado, peeled and seeded
Dipper

Soup	Seasoning 1	Seasoning 2	Dipper
cream of celery	1 tablespoon finely chopped onion	1 tablespoon chili powder	tortilla chips
cream of shrimp	1 tablespoon finely chopped shallots	2 teaspoons finely chopped, seeded jalapeño peppers	thinly sliced bagels, toasted
cream of chicken	1 clove garlic, minced	¼ teaspoon hot pepper sauce	assorted raw vegetables

In medium bowl with mixer at low speed, gradually beat **Soup** into cream cheese until smooth. Beat in **Seasoning 1** and **Seasoning 2**. Mash avocado; beat into soup mixture. Serve with **Dipper.** Makes about 2 cups.

Rumaki Spread

6 slices bacon
1 pound chicken livers
2 envelopes unflavored gelatin
Liquid
1 can (10¾ ounces) condensed **Soup**
¼ cup chopped water chestnuts
Flavoring
Accompaniment

Liquid	Soup	Flavoring	Accompaniment
¼ cup dry sherry plus ½ cup water	cream of onion	¼ cup chopped green onions	party rye rounds
¼ cup dry white wine plus ½ cup water	cream of celery	2 hard-cooked eggs, chopped	melba toast
¾ cup water	cream of mushroom	2 tablespoons chopped fresh chives	wheat crackers
¾ cup apple juice	cream of chicken	1 teaspoon curry powder	sliced French bread

1. In 10-inch skillet over medium heat, cook bacon until browned. Remove from skillet; drain on paper towels. Crumble and set aside.

2. Add chicken livers to pan drippings; cook until livers are tender, but still pink inside, stirring frequently. Remove from heat.

3. In small saucepan, sprinkle gelatin over **Liquid** to soften. Over low heat, heat until gelatin dissolves, stirring often. Remove from heat.

4. In food processor or blender container, combine **Soup,** cooked chicken livers and gelatin mixture. Process or blend until smooth. Pour into medium bowl. Stir in bacon, water chestnuts and **Flavoring.** Pour into 3-cup mold. Cover; refrigerate until set, at least 4 hours.

5. Unmold onto serving platter; serve with **Accompaniment.** Makes 16 appetizer servings.

Cheese-Stuffed Vegetables

1 can (10½ to 10¾ ounces) condensed **Soup**
1 package (8 ounces) cream cheese, softened
1 to 2 tablespoons lemon juice
1 clove garlic, minced
½ teaspoon **Herb,** crushed
¼ teaspoon **Spice**
Vegetables
Chopped fresh parsley

Soup	Herb	Spice	Vegetables
cream of onion	summer savory leaves	pepper	cherry tomatoes, tops and centers removed
cream of celery	tarragon leaves	ground nutmeg	celery stalks, cut into 2-inch pieces
cream of mushroom	thyme leaves	paprika	snow pea pods, cut open

1. In medium bowl with mixer at low speed, beat **Soup** into cream cheese until well blended. Beat in lemon juice, garlic, **Herb** and **Spice.** Cover; refrigerate until serving time, at least 4 hours.

2. Using a spoon or decorating tube, stuff cheese mixture into **Vegetables.** Sprinkle with parsley. Makes about 2¼ cups filling, 36 appetizers.

Tip: *To prepare cherry tomatoes for stuffing, slice off the tops, then scoop out the seeds and pulp with a small spoon or grapefruit knife. With a sharp knife, cut a decorative edge, if desired. To prepare pea pods for stuffing, make a slit in one long edge with a sharp knife.*

Mexican-Style Appetizer

1 can (11½ ounces) condensed bean with bacon soup
1 package (1¼ ounces) taco seasoning mix
¼ teaspoon hot pepper sauce
1 cup sour cream
1 can (4 ounces) chopped green chilies, drained
½ cup **Flavoring**
1 cup shredded **Cheese**
½ cup **Topper**
½ cup chopped tomato
Dipper

Flavoring	Cheese	Topper	Dipper
sliced pimento-stuffed olives	longhorn	alfalfa sprouts	tortilla chips
diced cooked ham	Monterey Jack	chopped green pepper	pita bread, torn and toasted
diced avocado	Cheddar	shredded lettuce	celery sticks
diced pepperoni	mozzarella	chopped celery with leaves	sliced jícama

1. In small bowl, combine soup with taco seasoning mix and hot pepper sauce; stir until blended. On large serving plate, spread mixture into a 6-inch round. Spread sides and top of bean mixture with sour cream to cover.

2. Layer chilies, **Flavoring, Cheese, Topper** and tomato over sour cream. Cover; refrigerate until serving time, at least 4 hours. Surround with **Dipper**. Makes 10 appetizer servings.

Tip: *Jícama is a Mexican vegetable that is becoming more readily available in U.S. markets. It is shaped like a turnip, has a brown skin, and may be cooked or eaten raw. To prepare, simply peel jícama and cut into thin slices or strips.*

Tomato Cheese Fondue

2 tablespoons butter or margarine
1 cup chopped tomatoes
½ cup chopped onion
1 clove garlic, minced
1 can (10¾ to 11 ounces) condensed **Soup**
Seasoning
Cheese, shredded
Dipper

Soup	Seasoning	Cheese	Dipper
cream of mushroom	½ teaspoon oregano leaves, crushed	1½ pounds sharp Cheddar	French bread cubes
cream of onion	½ teaspoon marjoram leaves, crushed	1 pound natural Swiss	celery sticks
cream of celery	⅛ teaspoon hot pepper sauce	1½ pounds Gruyère	corn chips
Cheddar cheese	¼ teaspoon dry mustard	1½ pounds Monterey Jack	apple wedges

1. In 3-quart saucepan over medium heat, in hot butter, cook tomatoes, onion and garlic 10 minutes or until mixture is slightly thickened, stirring often.

2. Stir in **Soup** and **Seasoning.** Gradually add **Cheese,** stirring until smooth after each addition.

3. Pour cheese mixture into fondue pot and keep warm. Serve with **Dipper.** Makes about 3½ cups.

To Microwave: In 2-quart microwave-safe casserole, combine butter, tomatoes, onion and garlic; cover. Microwave on HIGH 3 to 4 minutes until onion is tender, stirring once. Stir in **Soup, Seasoning** and **Cheese.** Microwave on HIGH 4 to 6 minutes until cheese melts, stirring occasionally. Proceed as in Step 3.

Tip: *If fondue becomes too thick, stir in a little milk.*

French Pizza Slices

½ pound bulk pork sausage
½ cup chopped onion
1 clove garlic, minced
1 can (10¾ ounces) condensed tomato soup
Vegetable
½ teaspoon **Herb,** crushed
Seasoning
1 loaf (12 to 14 inches) French bread, halved lengthwise
1 cup shredded **Cheese**

Vegetable	Herb	Seasoning	Cheese
½ cup sliced mushrooms	oregano leaves	few drops hot pepper sauce	mozzarella
½ cup chopped green pepper	basil leaves	1 teaspoon chili powder	Cheddar
½ cup sliced pitted ripe olives	marjoram leaves	2 tablespoons grated Romano cheese	American
¼ cup chopped green chilies	Italian seasoning	½ teaspoon ground cumin	Monterey Jack

1. In 10-inch skillet over medium heat, cook sausage, onion and garlic until vegetables are tender and sausage is well browned, stirring occasionally to break up meat. Pour off fat.

2. Add soup, **Vegetable, Herb** and **Seasoning.** Heat to boiling; reduce heat to low. Simmer, uncovered, 5 minutes. Remove from heat; cool slightly.

3. Arrange bread cut side up on baking sheet. Spoon soup mixture on bread; sprinkle with **Cheese.** Bake at 450°F. 15 minutes or until hot. Cut each bread half into 8 slices to serve. Makes 16 appetizers.

Tip: *To make ahead, prepare as above, but do not bake. Freeze until firm. When frozen, wrap in foil; return to freezer. Unwrap; place frozen bread on baking sheet. Bake at 450°F. 20 to 25 minutes until heated through.*

Soups

Chili

1 pound **Meat**
1 cup chopped onion
1 cup chopped green pepper
2 cloves garlic, minced
2 cans (10½ to 10¾ ounces each) condensed **Soup**
1 can (about 15 ounces) **Vegetable**
2 tablespoons chili powder
1 tablespoon vinegar
Garnish

Meat	Soup	Vegetable	Garnish
ground beef	tomato rice	kidney beans	shredded Cheddar cheese
bulk pork sausage	Spanish style vegetable	mixed vegetables	green pepper rings
Italian sausage, casings removed	tomato bisque	garbanzo beans	sour cream and sliced green onions
ground pork	tomato	whole kernel corn	crushed corn chips

1. In 4-quart Dutch oven over medium heat, cook **Meat,** onion, green pepper and garlic until meat is browned and vegetables are tender, stirring occasionally to break up meat. Pour off fat.

2. Stir in **Soup, Vegetable** and its liquid, chili powder and vinegar. Heat to boiling. Reduce heat to low; simmer, uncovered, 30 minutes, stirring occasionally.

3. Ladle into bowls; top with **Garnish.** Makes about 6½ cups, 6 servings.

To Microwave: In 2-quart microwave-safe casserole, crumble **Meat.** Add onion, green pepper and garlic; cover. Microwave on HIGH 7 to 9 minutes until meat is nearly done, stirring occasionally. Pour off fat. Stir in **Soup, Vegetable** and its liquid, chili powder and vinegar; cover. Microwave on HIGH 12 to 15 minutes until heated through, stirring occasionally. Ladle into bowls; top with **Garnish.**

Pasta and Bean Soup

Meat
½ cup chopped onion
½ cup chopped celery
½ cup shredded carrot
1 clove garlic, minced
1 can (10½ ounces) condensed **Soup**
1 soup can water
1 can (19 ounces) white kidney beans
½ teaspoon **Herb,** crushed
1 bay leaf
⅛ teaspoon pepper
½ cup uncooked **Pasta**

Meat	Soup	Herb	Pasta
½ cup diced cooked ham plus 2 tablespoons salad oil	vegetable	thyme leaves	small shell macaroni
4 slices bacon, diced	Spanish style vegetable	oregano leaves	ditalini
4 ounces bulk pork sausage, crumbled	minestrone	basil leaves	elbow macaroni

1. In 4-quart Dutch oven over medium heat, cook **Meat** until lightly browned, stirring occasionally. Add onion, celery, carrot and garlic; cook until vegetables are tender, stirring occasionally.

2. Stir in **Soup,** water, beans with their liquid, **Herb,** bay leaf and pepper. Heat to boiling. Reduce heat to low. Cover; simmer 15 minutes.

3. Stir in **Pasta;** cook about 12 minutes more or until pasta is tender. Discard bay leaf. Makes about 5 cups, 4 servings.

Tip: *Ditalini is a type of macaroni that is often included in Italian soups. It is shaped like short tubes.*

Easy Pea Soup

1 cup diced potato
½ cup chopped onion
Vegetable
Herb
1 cup chicken broth
½ cup water
1 can (11¼ ounces) condensed green pea soup
½ cup **Liquid**
Garnish

Vegetable	Herb	Liquid	Garnish
1 cup carrots cut into julienne strips	½ teaspoon summer savory leaves, crushed	half-and-half	sour cream
1 cup sliced celery	1 tablespoon chopped fresh parsley	milk	crumbled cooked bacon
1 large tomato, chopped	½ teaspoon oregano leaves, crushed	additional water	fresh mint leaves
1 cup fresh or frozen peas	¼ teaspoon rubbed sage	additional chicken broth	seasoned croutons

1. In 2-quart saucepan over medium heat, heat potato, onion, **Vegetable, Herb,** chicken broth and water to boiling. Reduce heat to low. Cover; simmer 10 minutes or until vegetables are tender.

2. Meanwhile, in medium bowl, combine pea soup and **Liquid;** stir until smooth. Add to broth mixture. Heat through. Ladle into bowls; top with **Garnish.** Makes about 4 cups, 4 servings.

To Microwave: In 2-quart microwave-safe casserole, combine potato, onion, **Vegetable, Herb,** chicken broth and water; cover. Microwave on HIGH 8 to 10 minutes until vegetables are tender, stirring once. Meanwhile, in medium bowl, combine pea soup and **Liquid;** stir until smooth. Add to broth mixture; cover. Microwave on HIGH 4 to 6 minutes until heated through, stirring once. Ladle into bowls; top with **Garnish.**

Tip: *To make seasoned croutons, cut 2 slices bread into ½-inch cubes. In small skillet, melt 1 tablespoon butter or margarine; stir in bread cubes. Cook over medium heat until bread is browned, stirring often. Toss with 1 tablespoon grated Parmesan cheese.*

Extra-Good Cream Soup

2 tablespoons butter or margarine
½ cup chopped onion
Vegetable
½ teaspoon **Herb,** crushed
1 can (10½ to 10¾ ounces) condensed **Soup**
½ cup light cream
¾ cup milk
Garnish

Vegetable	Herb	Soup	Garnish
1 medium tomato, diced	tarragon leaves	tomato	grated Parmesan cheese
1 cup sliced mushrooms	thyme leaves	cream of mushroom	chopped fresh parsley
1 cup fresh or frozen cut asparagus	dill weed	cream of asparagus	oyster crackers
1 cup sliced celery	marjoram leaves	cream of celery	melba toast

1. In 2-quart saucepan over medium heat, in hot butter, cook onion, **Vegetable** and **Herb** until vegetables are tender, stirring occasionally.

2. Stir in **Soup,** cream and milk. Heat through, stirring occasionally. Ladle into bowls; serve with **Garnish.** Makes about 3½ cups, 4 servings.

To Microwave: In 2-quart microwave-safe casserole, combine butter, onion, **Vegetable** and **Herb;** cover. Microwave on HIGH 7 to 9 minutes until vegetables are tender, stirring once. Stir in **Soup,** cream and milk; cover. Microwave on HIGH 5 to 7 minutes until heated through, stirring occasionally. Ladle into bowls; serve with **Garnish.**

Tip: *Here's an extra-quick, extra-good chicken and corn soup: In medium saucepan, stir 1 can (10¾ ounces) condensed cream of chicken soup. Stir in 1 soup can milk, 1 can (5 ounces) chunk white chicken and 1 can (8 ounces) whole kernel corn. Heat to simmering, stirring often.*

Speedy Potato Chowder

4 slices bacon, diced
½ cup chopped onion
1 can (10¾ ounces) condensed cream of potato soup
Liquid
1 can (about 8 ounces) **Vegetable**
Meat
2 tablespoons chopped fresh parsley

Liquid	Vegetable	Meat
¾ cup beer plus ¾ cup water	mixed vegetables	1 cup sliced frankfurters
1½ cups milk	whole kernel corn	1 cup diced cooked chicken
1 cup milk plus ½ cup light cream	lima beans	1 cup diced cooked ham
1 cup evaporated milk plus ½ cup water	diced carrots	1 can (about 7 ounces) tuna, drained and flaked

1. In 3-quart saucepan over medium heat, cook bacon until crisp. Remove with slotted spoon and drain on paper towels. Pour off all but 1 tablespoon bacon drippings.

2. In hot drippings, cook onion until tender, stirring occasionally. Stir in soup and **Liquid** until well mixed. Add **Vegetable** with its liquid, **Meat,** parsley and reserved bacon. Heat through, stirring occasionally. Makes about 4 cups, 4 servings.

To Microwave: In 2-quart microwave-safe casserole, place bacon; cover. Microwave on HIGH 3 to 4 minutes until crisp, stirring once. With slotted spoon, remove bacon; drain on paper towels. Pour off all but 1 tablespoon bacon drippings. To drippings, add onion; cover. Microwave on HIGH 2 to 2½ minutes until tender, stirring once. Stir in soup and **Liquid** until well mixed. Add **Vegetable** with its liquid, **Meat,** parsley and reserved bacon; cover. Microwave on HIGH 8 to 10 minutes until heated through, stirring occasionally.

Tip: *If you don't have leftover ham or chicken, buy it already cooked at your supermarket's delicatessen. You'll need about 5 ounces cooked chicken or ham to make 1 cup diced.*

Skillet Seafood Bisque

¼ cup butter or margarine
1 cup sliced mushrooms
Vegetable
1 clove garlic, minced
3 tablespoons all-purpose flour
1 can (10¾ ounces) condensed chicken broth
Seafood
Liquid
1 tablespoon chopped fresh parsley
Garnish

Vegetable	Seafood	Liquid	Garnish
2 tablespoons chopped fresh chives	1 pound medium shrimp, shelled and deveined	½ cup dry white wine plus ½ cup heavy cream	fresh dill sprigs
¼ cup chopped onion	1 pound bay scallops	1 cup half-and-half	grated Parmesan cheese
¼ cup chopped green onions	1 pound monkfish or other firm fish fillets, cubed	1 cup milk	ground nutmeg
½ cup chopped green pepper	1 pint shucked clams, drained and chopped	1 cup clam juice	cooked, crumbled bacon

1. In 10-inch skillet over medium heat, in hot butter, cook mushrooms, **Vegetable** and garlic until vegetables are tender, stirring occasionally. Stir in flour until smooth. Gradually stir in chicken broth. Heat to boiling, stirring constantly.

2. Add **Seafood.** Reduce heat to low. Cover; simmer about 5 minutes or until seafood is done. Stir in **Liquid** and parsley; heat through. Ladle into bowls; top with **Garnish.** Makes about 4½ cups, 6 servings.

Tip: *Here's a speedy seafood soup: In medium saucepan, stir 1 can (10¾ ounces) condensed cream of mushroom soup. Stir in 1 soup can milk and 1 can (6½ ounces) minced clams with their liquid. Heat to simmering, stirring often.*

Fish Stew

¼ cup salad oil
1 cup chopped onion
1 cup **Vegetable 1**
3 cloves garlic, minced
2 cans (10½ to 10¾ ounces each) condensed **Soup**
1 soup can water
1 can (6 ounces) tomato paste
Vegetable 2
1 bay leaf
Herb, crushed
2 pounds haddock or other fish fillets, cut into 1½-inch pieces
½ pound medium shrimp, shelled and deveined
12 medium clams in shells or 1 can (6½ ounces) minced clams

Vegetable 1	Soup	Vegetable 2	Herb
chopped green pepper	chicken broth	1 can (16 ounces) tomatoes, cut up (do not drain)	1 teaspoon basil leaves
chopped celery and celery leaves	chicken vegetable	2 cups diced peeled potatoes	½ teaspoon tarragon leaves
chopped zucchini	chicken gumbo	2 cups cubed eggplant	½ teaspoon oregano leaves
shredded carrot	chicken with rice	2 cups fresh or frozen whole kernel corn	1 teaspoon dill weed

1. In 5-quart Dutch oven over medium heat, in hot oil, cook onion, **Vegetable 1** and garlic until vegetables are tender, stirring occasionally.

2. Stir in **Soup,** water, tomato paste, **Vegetable 2,** bay leaf and **Herb.** Heat to boiling. Reduce heat; simmer, uncovered, 15 minutes.

3. Add fish, shrimp and clams. Cover; simmer 10 minutes or until fish flakes easily when tested with fork and clam shells are opened (discard any clams that do not open). Discard bay leaf. Makes about 10 cups, 8 servings.

Soup Mates

One easy way to create a new soup is to combine two different condensed soups. Over the years, we have experimented with hundreds of combinations; here are some of our favorites.

To prepare soup mates, simply empty the soups into a saucepan. Gradually stir in the liquid; heat to simmer, stirring occasionally.

Soup 1		Soup 2		Liquid
split pea with ham & bacon	+	cream of celery	+	1 can milk plus 1 can water
golden mushroom	+	French onion	+	1 can milk plus 1 can water
tomato	+	green pea	+	1 can milk plus 1 can water
Cheddar cheese	+	cream of asparagus	+	1 can milk plus 1 can water
chicken noodle	+	chicken & stars	+	2 cans water
New England clam chowder	+	cream of mushroom	+	1 can milk plus 1 can water
bean with bacon	+	tomato rice	+	2 cans water
chicken gumbo	+	cream of celery	+	1 can milk plus 1 can water
Cheddar cheese	+	tomato	+	1 can milk plus 1 can water
chili beef	+	vegetable beef	+	2 cans water
cream of chicken	+	green pea	+	1 can milk plus 1 can water
black bean	+	golden mushroom	+	2 cans water
tomato	+	beef noodle	+	2 cans water
cream of celery	+	vegetarian vegetable	+	1 can milk plus 1 can water
oyster stew	+	cream of potato	+	2 cans milk
cream of mushroom	+	beef broth	+	2 cans water
minestrone	+	Manhattan clam chowder	+	2 cans water
turkey noodle	+	cream of celery	+	1 can milk plus 1 can water
meatball alphabet	+	Cheddar cheese	+	1 can milk plus 1 can water
cream of mushroom	+	tomato	+	1 can milk plus 1 can water
bean with bacon	+	French onion	+	2 cans water
chicken vegetable	+	cream of chicken	+	1 can milk plus 1 can water
New England clam chowder	+	cream of asparagus	+	2 cans milk
chicken gumbo	+	vegetable	+	2 cans water

Main Dishes

Fruited Chops

2 tablespoons salad oil
1½ pounds **Chops**, each cut ½ inch thick
1 can (10¾ ounces) condensed chicken broth
2 tablespoons soy sauce
1 tablespoon vinegar
Fruit
2 tablespoons brown sugar
2 tablespoons cornstarch
1 teaspoon ground **Spice**
Hot cooked rice
Garnish

Chops	Fruit	Spice	Garnish
pork	1 large apple, cubed, plus ½ cup apple juice	ginger	sliced green onion
lamb	4 orange slices, cut up, plus ½ cup orange juice	nutmeg	slivered orange peel
smoked pork	1 can (8 ounces) pineapple slices, cut up	mace	chopped fresh parsley
veal	1 can (8 ounces) apricot halves, cut up	cinnamon	sliced water chestnuts

1. In 10-inch skillet over medium-high heat, in hot oil, cook **Chops** until browned on both sides.

2. Stir in chicken broth, soy sauce and vinegar. Heat to boiling; reduce heat to low. Cover; simmer 20 minutes or until chops are tender.

3. Meanwhile, drain **Fruit,** reserving liquid. Add enough water to liquid to make ½ cup, if necessary. In small bowl, combine liquid, brown sugar, cornstarch and **Spice;** stir until smooth.

4. Remove chops from skillet; keep warm. Stir cornstarch mixture into skillet. Over medium heat, heat to boiling. Add reserved fruit; heat through.

5. Arrange chops over rice; spoon sauce over chops. Top with **Garnish.** Makes 4 servings.

Easy Pot Roast

Fat
3½-pound beef chuck pot roast
1 can (10¾ ounces) condensed **Soup**
Herb
2 tablespoons all-purpose flour
¼ cup **Liquid**

Fat	Soup	Herb	Liquid
2 tablespoons shortening	cream of onion	1 teaspoon thyme leaves, crushed	water
2 tablespoons salad oil	cream of mushroom	1 teaspoon rosemary leaves, crushed	dry white wine
non-stick cooking spray	cream of celery	1 teaspoon marjoram leaves, crushed	heavy cream
2 tablespoons bacon drippings	golden mushroom	1 bay leaf (remove before serving)	dry red wine

1. In 6-quart Dutch oven over medium-high heat, in hot **Fat,** brown beef on all sides. Pour off fat.

2. Stir in **Soup** and **Herb.** Reduce heat to low. Cover; simmer 2½ to 3 hours until tender, stirring occasionally. Add water during cooking, if necessary.

3. Remove beef to platter; keep warm. In screw-top jar, shake together flour and **Liquid** until smooth; stir into pan drippings. Over high heat, heat to boiling, stirring constantly. Cook 1 minute more.

4. Cut meat into thin slices. Serve gravy with meat. Makes 8 servings.

Tip: *The cooking time needed for a pot roast depends on its shape as well as on its size. Thin roasts such as underblade roast need less time; blocky roasts such as shoulder roast need more.*

Garden Swiss Steak

¼ cup all-purpose flour
1 pound beef round steak, cut ½ inch thick
2 tablespoons salad oil
1 clove garlic, minced
1 bay leaf
⅛ teaspoon pepper
1 can (10¾ ounces) condensed **Soup**
½ cup water
1 medium green pepper, cut into strips
Vegetable 1
½ cup **Vegetable 2**
Accompaniment

Soup	Vegetable 1	Vegetable 2	Accompaniment
tomato	1 medium onion, sliced	sliced mushrooms	hot mashed potatoes
cream of onion	1 cup sliced zucchini	sliced carrots	hot buttered noodles
cream of mushroom	6 green onions, sliced	chopped tomatoes	hot cooked rice
cream of potato	1 cup sliced celery	sliced parsnips	hot biscuits

1. On cutting board with meat mallet, pound flour into both sides of steak until all flour is absorbed and meat is slightly flattened. Cut steak into 4 serving-size pieces. In 10-inch skillet over medium-high heat, in hot oil, cook steak until browned on both sides.

2. Add garlic, bay leaf and pepper. Spoon **Soup** over meat; add water. Heat to boiling. Reduce heat to low. Cover; simmer 1 hour, stirring occasionally.

3. Add green pepper, **Vegetable 1** and **Vegetable 2.** Cover; simmer 30 minutes more or until meat is tender. Discard bay leaf. Serve with **Accompaniment.** Makes 4 servings.

Tip: *When using celery, chop a few celery leaves and add them to the skillet for extra flavor.*

Stir-Fried Beef and Vegetables

½ pound boneless beef sirloin steak
1 can (10½ to 10¾ ounces) condensed **Soup**
1 tablespoon cornstarch
1 tablespoon soy sauce
3 tablespoons salad oil
1 clove garlic, minced
4 green onions, cut into 1-inch pieces
1 cup **Vegetable 1**
Vegetable 2
Accompaniment

Soup	Vegetable 1	Vegetable 2	Accompaniment
beef broth	fresh or frozen cut broccoli	1 can (8 ounces) sliced bamboo shoots, drained	shredded lettuce
French onion	sliced mushrooms	1 cup diced tomatoes	hot cooked rice
chicken broth	fresh or frozen cut asparagus	1 can (8 ounces) sliced water chestnuts, drained	hot cooked noodles
chicken with rice	sliced celery	1 cup fresh or canned bean sprouts	chow mein noodles

1. Freeze steak 1 hour to make slicing easier. Trim and discard excess fat from steak. Cut steak into very thin slices; set aside.

2. In small bowl, combine **Soup,** cornstarch and soy sauce; stir to blend. Set aside.

3. In 10-inch skillet or wok over medium-high heat, in 2 tablespoons hot oil, stir-fry beef strips and garlic until meat is browned; remove from skillet.

4. Add remaining 1 tablespoon oil to skillet. Add green onions and **Vegetable 1;** stir-fry 1 minute. Add **Vegetable 2;** stir-fry 30 seconds more.

5. Return beef to skillet. Stir soup mixture; stir into skillet. Heat to boiling; cook 1 minute more. Spoon over **Accompaniment.** Makes about 2½ cups, 2 servings.

Tip: *To make delicious sandwiches, spoon beef mixture into pita bread halves; omit* **Accompaniment.**

Teriyaki Beef Kabobs

1 can (10½ to 11 ounces) condensed **Soup**
¼ cup dry sherry
¼ cup soy sauce
1 large clove garlic, minced
Seasoning
1 tablespoon **Sweetener**
1½ pounds boneless beef sirloin steak, cut 1 inch thick
1 medium green pepper, cut into 1-inch squares
1 pound small whole onions, cooked and drained
½ cup pineapple chunks
Accompaniment

Soup	Seasoning	Sweetener	Accompaniment
Spanish style vegetable	¼ cup sliced green onions	honey	hot cooked rice
French onion	¼ cup finely chopped onion	brown sugar	hot cooked wild rice
beef broth	½ teaspoon ground ginger	sugar	hot cooked bulgur wheat
tomato bisque	1 teaspoon dry mustard	molasses	hot cooked noodles

1. For marinade, in medium bowl, combine **Soup,** sherry, soy sauce, garlic, **Seasoning** and **Sweetener.**

2. Cut beef into 1-inch cubes; add to marinade. Cover; refrigerate 3 hours or overnight, turning once or twice.

3. Drain meat, reserving marinade. Thread beef cubes, green pepper, onions and pineapple chunks on six 12-inch skewers.

4. On rack in broiler pan, broil 6 inches from heat 10 minutes or until meat is cooked to desired doneness, turning and brushing often with marinade. Serve with **Accompaniment.** Makes 6 servings.

Tip: *Assemble skewers before marinating. Place in shallow dish; pour marinade over skewers. Cover; refrigerate 3 hours or overnight, turning occasionally.*

Best-Ever Meat Loaf

1 can (10¾ to 11 ounces) condensed **Soup**
Meat
Crumbs
1 egg, beaten
⅓ cup finely chopped onion
Seasoning
⅓ cup water

Soup	Meat	Crumbs	Seasoning
golden mushroom	2 pounds ground beef	½ cup fine dry bread crumbs	1 tablespoon Worcestershire
cream of mushroom	2 pounds meat loaf mix (beef, pork, veal)	½ cup quick-cooking oats	1 tablespoon soy sauce
Cheddar cheese	1½ pounds ground beef plus ½ pound Italian sausage, casings removed	½ cup finely crushed saltines	¼ cup chopped pimento-stuffed olives

1. In large bowl, thoroughly mix ½ cup of the **Soup, Meat, Crumbs,** egg, onion and **Seasoning.** In 12 by 8-inch baking pan, firmly shape meat into 8 by 4-inch loaf.

2. Bake at 350°F. 1¼ hours or until done. Remove meat loaf to platter; keep warm.

3. Pour off all but 3 tablespoons drippings from pan. Stir remaining **Soup** and water into drippings in pan, scraping up brown bits from bottom. Over medium heat, heat soup mixture until hot, stirring constantly. Serve gravy with meat loaf. Makes 8 servings.

Tip: *If you use a glass baking dish for your meat loaf, prepare as above in steps 1 and 2. Pour 3 tablespoons drippings into a small saucepan; discard remaining drippings. Stir remaining* **Soup** *and water into saucepan. Over medium heat, heat soup mixture until hot, stirring constantly. Serve as above.*

Stuffed Cabbage Leaves

1 pound **Meat**
½ cup chopped onion
1 can (10½ ounces) condensed beef broth
½ cup **Grain**
½ teaspoon grated lemon peel
½ cup **Fruit**
¼ cup chopped walnuts
¼ cup chopped fresh parsley
½ teaspoon dried mint leaves (optional)
1 medium head cabbage
1 can (10½ to 11 ounces) condensed **Soup**
¼ teaspoon ground cinnamon

Meat	Grain	Fruit	Soup
ground pork	raw bulgur wheat	chopped apple	tomato plus 1 tablespoon lemon juice
ground lamb	raw brown rice	golden raisins	Spanish style vegetable
ground beef	raw regular rice	chopped dried apricots	tomato rice plus 1 tablespoon lemon juice

1. In 10-inch skillet over medium heat, cook **Meat** and onion until meat is well browned, stirring occasionally to break up meat. Pour off fat.

2. Add beef broth, **Grain** and lemon peel. Heat to boiling. Reduce heat to low. Cover; simmer until grain is tender, about 45 minutes for brown rice or 20 to 25 minutes for regular rice or bulgur; add a little water during cooking if mixture becomes dry. Remove from heat. Stir in **Fruit,** walnuts, parsley and mint.

3. Meanwhile, in 4-quart saucepan over high heat, heat about 6 cups water to boiling. Add whole head of cabbage to boiling water. Reduce heat to low. Cover; simmer 1 to 2 minutes or until outer leaves are softened. Remove cabbage from water. Carefully remove 6 outer leaves. Reserve remaining cabbage for another use.

4. Drain cabbage leaves on paper towels. Lay leaves flat on cutting board and cut out any tough stems. Spoon about ¾ cup meat filling into center of one leaf. Fold in sides, then roll up from stem end to form a bundle. Repeat with remaining leaves and filling.

5. In medium bowl, stir together **Soup** and cinnamon. Pour ½ of the soup mixture into 12 by 8-inch baking dish. Place cabbage rolls seam side down in prepared dish. Pour remaining soup mixture over all. Cover with foil. Bake at 350°F. 35 minutes or until heated through. Makes 6 servings.

Tacos

Meat
½ cup chopped onion
2 cloves garlic, minced
1 tablespoon chili powder
1 can (10½ to 11 ounces) condensed **Soup**
8 taco shells
1 cup shredded **Cheese**
Shredded lettuce
1 cup **Addition**

Meat	Soup	Cheese	Addition
1 pound ground beef	tomato	Cheddar	chopped tomatoes
1 pound ground pork	tomato rice	longhorn	diced avocado
1½ cups chopped cooked beef plus 2 tablespoons salad oil	Spanish style vegetable	Monterey Jack	chopped green onions
1 pound bulk pork sausage	tomato bisque	American	salsa

1. Preheat oven to 350°F. In 10-inch skillet over medium heat, cook **Meat,** onion, garlic and chili powder until meat is well browned, stirring to break up meat. Pour off fat. Stir in **Soup.** Heat through, stirring occasionally.

2. Place about ¼ cup meat mixture in each taco shell. Place on baking sheet. Bake 5 minutes. Top with **Cheese,** lettuce and **Addition.** Makes 8 tacos, 4 servings.

To Microwave: In 1½-quart microwave-safe casserole, crumble **Meat.** Add onion, garlic and chili powder; cover. Microwave on HIGH 6 to 8 minutes until meat is nearly done, stirring occasionally. Pour off fat. Stir in **Soup;** cover. Microwave on HIGH 2 to 3 minutes until heated through, stirring once. Place about ¼ cup meat mixture in each taco shell. In 12 by 8-inch microwave-safe dish, arrange taco shells. Microwave on HIGH 2 to 3 minutes. Top with **Cheese,** lettuce and **Addition.**

Souper Enchiladas

½ cup salad oil
8 corn tortillas (6-inch)
1 cup chopped onion
1 large clove garlic, minced
1 can (11 to 11½ ounces) condensed **Soup**
2 cups shredded cooked **Meat**
½ cup water
1 teaspoon ground cumin
Seasoning
1 jar (8 ounces) taco sauce
1 cup shredded **Cheese**

Soup	Meat	Seasoning	Cheese
black bean	chicken	1 can (4 ounces) chopped green chilies, drained	Cheddar
bean with bacon	pork	2 jalapeño peppers, seeded and chopped	longhorn
chili beef	beef	¼ teaspoon hot pepper sauce	Monterey Jack

1. In 8-inch skillet over medium heat, in hot oil, fry tortillas, one at a time, 2 to 3 seconds on each side. Drain tortillas on paper towels.

2. Spoon about 2 tablespoons of the hot oil into 10-inch skillet. Over medium heat, in the 2 tablespoons oil, cook onion and garlic until tender, stirring occasionally. Stir in **Soup, Meat,** water, cumin and **Seasoning.** Heat through.

3. Spoon about ⅓ cup soup mixture onto each tortilla; roll up. Arrange filled tortillas in 12 by 8-inch baking dish. Pour taco sauce evenly over enchiladas. Sprinkle with **Cheese.** Cover with foil.

4. Bake at 350°F. 25 minutes. Uncover; bake 5 minutes more. Makes 4 servings.

To Microwave: Use ingredients as above but use only 1 tablespoon oil. In 2-quart microwave-safe casserole, combine only 1 tablespoon oil, onion and garlic; cover. Microwave on HIGH 2 to 3 minutes until tender. Stir in **Soup, Meat,** water, cumin and **Seasoning;** cover. Microwave on HIGH 4 to 6 minutes until heated through, stirring once. Let stand, covered. Meanwhile, wrap tortillas in paper towel and place in microwave oven. Microwave on HIGH 2 minutes or until tortillas are pliable. Assemble as in Step 3, placing filled tortillas in 12 by 8-inch microwave-safe dish. Pour taco sauce evenly over enchiladas; cover. Microwave on HIGH 8 to 10 minutes until hot, rotating dish once. Sprinkle with **Cheese.** Microwave on HIGH 2 to 3 minutes until cheese is melted.

Meatball Stew

1 pound ground beef
Crumbs
½ teaspoon **Herb,** crushed
1 egg
1 clove garlic, minced
2 tablespoons salad oil
1 can (10½ to 11 ounces) condensed **Soup**
¼ cup water
3 medium potatoes, peeled and quartered
Vegetable
1 medium onion, cut into thin wedges
1 tablespoon chopped fresh parsley

Crumbs	Herb	Soup	Vegetable
½ cup soft bread crumbs	summer savory leaves	French onion	3 medium carrots, cut into 1-inch chunks
¼ cup seasoned fine dry bread crumbs	basil leaves	tomato bisque	1½ cups celery cut into ½-inch chunks
¼ cup finely crushed saltines	oregano leaves	vegetable beef	1½ cups cut green beans
¼ cup quick-cooking oats	thyme leaves	Spanish style vegetable	3 medium parsnips, peeled and cut into 1-inch chunks

1. In medium bowl, combine ground beef, **Crumbs, Herb,** egg and garlic; mix thoroughly. Shape into 20 meatballs.

2. In 10-inch skillet over medium heat, in hot oil, cook meatballs until browned on all sides. Pour off fat.

3. Stir **Soup** and water into skillet; stir in potatoes, **Vegetable** and onion. Heat to boiling. Reduce heat to low. Cover; simmer 30 minutes or until vegetables are tender, adding more water if needed. Garnish with parsley. Makes 4 servings.

Tip: *Don't overmix meat mixture or meat will become tough.*

Chicken Paprika

2 tablespoons salad oil
2 pounds chicken parts
1 can (10¾ ounces) condensed **Soup**
Vegetable
1 medium onion, sliced and separated into rings
1 clove garlic, minced
2 teaspoons paprika
½ cup sour cream
Accompaniment

Soup	Vegetable	Accompaniment
cream of chicken	1 cup quartered mushrooms	hot cooked noodles
cream of onion	½ cup diced celery	hot cooked rice
cream of mushroom	1 cup chopped tomatoes	hot cooked wild rice
cream of celery	½ cup diced carrots	hot cooked kasha

1. In 10-inch skillet over medium heat, in hot oil, cook chicken until browned on all sides. Pour off fat. Stir in **Soup, Vegetable,** onion, garlic and paprika. Heat to boiling. Reduce heat to low. Cover; simmer 30 to 40 minutes until chicken is fork-tender.

2. Remove chicken to platter; keep warm. Stir sour cream into sauce; over low heat, heat through, stirring constantly. Spoon some of sauce over chicken. Serve chicken with **Accompaniment;** pass remaining sauce. Makes 4 servings.

Tip: *Kasha is a coarsely ground grain, usually buckwheat, that is prominent in Eastern European cuisines. Look for it near the rice or in the gourmet section of your supermarket.*

Chicken Breasts in Mushroom Sauce

3 whole chicken breasts, skinned, boned and split
⅓ cup all-purpose flour
2 tablespoons salad oil
2 tablespoons butter or margarine
1 clove garlic, halved
1 cup sliced mushrooms
Vegetable
1 can (10½ to 10¾ ounces) condensed **Soup**
¼ cup **Wine**
Dash pepper
Accompaniment

Vegetable	Soup	Wine	Accompaniment
¼ cup sliced green onions	chicken gumbo	dry vermouth	hot cooked rice
½ cup sliced celery	chicken with rice	dry sherry	hot mashed potatoes
½ cup shredded carrot	chicken broth	dry white wine	hot cooked noodles
¼ cup sliced leek	chicken vegetable	dry red wine	hot cooked bulgur wheat

1. With meat mallet, pound chicken to ¼-inch thickness. Coat with flour.

2. In 10-inch skillet over medium heat, in hot oil and butter, cook garlic 30 seconds; discard garlic.

3. Cook chicken cutlets, 2 or 3 at a time, until lightly browned on both sides; remove from skillet. Repeat with remaining cutlets.

4. Add mushrooms and **Vegetable** to skillet; cook until vegetables are tender, stirring occasionally. Stir in **Soup, Wine** and pepper, scraping bottom to loosen brown bits. Return cutlets to skillet. Reduce heat to low. Cover; simmer 15 minutes or until chicken is fork-tender. Serve cutlets with sauce and **Accompaniment.** Makes 6 servings.

Tip: *Bulgur is precooked cracked wheat that is most often found in health food stores or Middle Eastern food shops. If you have a choice, purchase the coarse grind for use with this recipe.*

Baked Chicken Florida

1 can (10½ to 10¾ ounces) condensed **Soup**
Juice
Seasoning
¼ teaspoon tarragon leaves, crushed
3 pounds chicken parts
1 tablespoon cornstarch
Garnish

Soup	Juice	Seasoning	Garnish
Spanish style vegetable	½ cup orange juice	½ teaspoon minced fresh ginger root	orange wedges
chicken broth	¼ cup lemon juice plus ¼ cup water	1 clove garlic, minced	avocado slices
chicken with rice	¼ cup lime juice plus ¼ cup water	2 tablespoons chopped fresh chives	kiwi fruit slices

1. For marinade, in small bowl, combine **Soup, Juice, Seasoning** and tarragon. In shallow baking dish, pour marinade over chicken. Cover; refrigerate at least 2 hours, turning chicken occasionally. Drain chicken, reserving marinade.

2. In shallow roasting pan, arrange chicken. Bake at 375°F. 50 minutes or until chicken is fork-tender, basting chicken frequently with marinade. Remove to serving platter; keep warm.

3. Pour remaining marinade and pan drippings into 1-quart saucepan; stir in cornstarch. Over medium heat, heat to boiling, stirring occasionally; cook 1 minute more. Spoon some sauce over chicken; pass remainder. Arrange **Garnish** around chicken. Makes 6 servings.

Tip: *A garnish of kiwi fruit can turn an ordinary dish into a picture-pretty one. To use kiwi, simply peel the brown skin with a vegetable peeler or paring knife, then cut the fruit into slices.*

Supper à la King

¼ cup butter or margarine
½ cup diced green pepper
⅓ cup chopped onion
1 can (10¾ ounces) condensed **Soup**
¾ cup milk
2 cups cubed cooked **Meat**
¾ cup shredded **Cheese**
¼ cup diced pimento
Accompaniment

Soup	Meat	Cheese	Accompaniment
cream of chicken	chicken	Swiss	shredded zucchini, cooked and drained
cream of asparagus	ham	Cheddar	baked potatoes, split
cream of mushroom	turkey	Muenster	cooked spaghetti squash (see **Tip** below)
cream of celery	kielbasa	American	biscuits, split

1. In 10-inch skillet over medium heat, in hot butter, cook green pepper and onion until tender, stirring occasionally. Stir in **Soup** and milk; blend well. Stir in **Meat, Cheese** and pimento. Cook 5 minutes more or until heated through.

2. Arrange **Accompaniment** on serving platter. Serve sauce over accompaniment. Makes about 3½ cups sauce, 6 servings.

To Microwave: Use ingredients as above but use only 2 tablespoons butter. In 2-quart microwave-safe casserole, combine only 2 tablespoons butter, green pepper and onion; cover. Microwave on HIGH 2 to 3 minutes until vegetables are tender. Stir in **Soup** and milk; blend well. Stir in **Meat, Cheese** and pimento; cover. Microwave on HIGH 7 to 9 minutes until heated through, stirring occasionally. Serve as above.

Tip: *To cook spaghetti squash: Halve squash lengthwise; remove seeds and stringy portions. In 10-inch skillet, place squash halves cut side up. Add 1 inch water. Over medium heat, heat to boiling. Reduce heat to low. Cover; simmer 30 minutes or until fork-tender. Drain. With fork, scrape spaghetti-like strands from squash shell; place on serving platter. Discard shells.*

Chicken-Stuffing Bake

1 cup water
¼ cup butter or margarine
1 package (7 ounces) seasoned stuffing mix
1 can (10¾ to 11 ounces) condensed **Soup**
½ cup mayonnaise
⅓ cup milk
2 cups diced cooked chicken or turkey
2 stalks celery, chopped
1 cup drained, cooked **Vegetable**
½ teaspoon **Seasoning**
Cheese

Soup	Vegetable	Seasoning	Cheese
cream of chicken	peas	thyme leaves, crushed	1 cup shredded Cheddar
cream of mushroom	mixed vegetables	marjoram leaves, crushed	1 cup shredded Swiss
cream of onion	chopped spinach	rubbed sage	1 cup shredded Monterey Jack
Cheddar cheese	chopped broccoli	poultry seasoning	¼ cup grated Parmesan

1. In 1-quart saucepan over high heat, heat water and butter to boiling. In large bowl, pour hot water mixture over stuffing mix; toss to mix well. Pat ½ of the stuffing mixture into 12 by 8-inch baking dish.

2. In medium bowl, stir together **Soup,** mayonnaise, milk, chicken, celery, **Vegetable** and **Seasoning** until well mixed. Spoon evenly over stuffing mixture in baking dish; top with remaining stuffing mixture.

3. Bake at 400°F. 30 minutes or until heated through. Sprinkle with **Cheese.** Bake 5 minutes more or until cheese is melted. Makes 6 servings.

To Microwave: Prepare as in Steps 1 and 2 but assemble in 12 by 8-inch microwave-safe dish; cover. Microwave on HIGH 8 to 10 minutes until heated through, rotating dish once. Sprinkle with **Cheese.** Microwave on HIGH 2 minutes or until cheese is melted.

Vegetable Lasagna

2 tablespoons olive or salad oil
1 large onion, chopped
1 clove garlic, minced
1 teaspoon Italian seasoning, crushed
Vegetable
1 can (10¾ to 11 ounces) condensed **Soup**
Cheese
1 egg
1 jar (32 ounces) spaghetti sauce
Liquid
9 lasagna noodles, cooked and drained
2 cups shredded mozzarella cheese

Vegetable	Soup	Cheese	Liquid
2 packages (10 ounces each) frozen chopped broccoli, thawed and drained	cream of chicken	2 cups shredded sharp Cheddar	½ cup dry red wine
2 packages (10 ounces each) frozen chopped spinach, thawed and drained	cream of mushroom	1 cup grated Parmesan	1 cup heavy cream
4 cups sliced zucchini	cream of celery	2 cups shredded Swiss	2 tablespoons vinegar plus ½ cup water
2 packages (9 ounces each) frozen cut green beans, thawed and drained	Cheddar cheese	1 cup ricotta plus ¼ cup crumbled blue cheese	½ cup plain yogurt

1. In 10-inch skillet over medium heat, in hot oil, cook onion, garlic and Italian seasoning until onion is tender, stirring occasionally. Stir in **Vegetable**; cook until vegetable is tender and liquid evaporates. Remove from heat; stir in **Soup, Cheese** and egg. Set filling aside.

2. In medium bowl, stir together spaghetti sauce and **Liquid**; pour ½ of the sauce mixture into 13 by 9-inch baking dish. Set remainder aside.

3. Arrange 3 lasagna noodles over sauce; spread with ½ of the vegetable filling. Sprinkle with ⅓ of the mozzarella. Arrange 3 more noodles over cheese; spread with remaining filling. Sprinkle with another ⅓ of the mozzarella. Top with remaining 3 noodles and remaining sauce.

4. Bake at 350°F. 40 minutes or until hot. Sprinkle with remaining ⅓ of the mozzarella; bake 5 minutes more. Let stand 15 minutes before serving. Makes 6 servings.

Vegetable-Stuffed Fish Rolls

½ cup chopped tomato
½ cup chopped mushrooms
¼ cup chopped green onions
1 can (10¾ to 11 ounces) condensed **Soup**
6 **Fish** fillets (1½ pounds)
¼ cup **Liquid**
1 cup shredded **Cheese**

Soup	Fish	Liquid	Cheese
cream of shrimp	flounder	dry sherry	Swiss
cream of mushroom	sole	dry white wine	Provolone
Cheddar cheese	perch	milk	sharp Cheddar
cream of celery	haddock	water	Muenster

1. In medium bowl, combine tomato, mushrooms, green onions and ¼ cup of the **Soup.** Place about 3 tablespoons of the mixture on each **Fish** fillet and roll up. Secure with toothpicks if needed. Place fish rolls seam side down in 10 by 6-inch baking dish. Bake at 350°F. 25 minutes or until fish flakes easily when tested with fork. Discard any liquid in baking dish.

2. Meanwhile, in 2-quart saucepan, combine remaining **Soup** and **Liquid.** Over medium heat, heat through. Pour sauce over fish rolls; sprinkle with **Cheese.**

3. Bake 2 minutes more or until cheese is melted. Makes 6 servings.

To Microwave: In medium bowl, combine tomato, mushrooms, green onions and ¼ cup of the **Soup.** Fill and roll **Fish** as directed. Place fish rolls seam side down in 10 by 6-inch microwave-safe dish; cover. Microwave on HIGH 8 to 14 minutes until fish flakes easily when tested with fork, rotating dish twice. Discard any liquid in dish. Let stand, covered, 2 to 3 minutes. Meanwhile, in 2-cup glass measure, combine remaining **Soup** and **Liquid.** Microwave on HIGH 2 minutes or until hot. Pour sauce over fish rolls; top with **Cheese.** Microwave on HIGH 1 minute more or until cheese is melted.

Perfect Tuna Casserole

1 can (10¾ ounces) condensed **Soup**
¼ cup milk
1 can (about 7 ounces) tuna, drained and flaked
2 hard-cooked eggs, sliced
1 cup drained, cooked **Vegetable**
Topper

Soup	Vegetable	Topper
cream of mushroom	peas	½ cup coarsely crumbled potato chips
cream of onion	cut green beans	3 slices American cheese, cut into slivers
cream of shrimp	cut broccoli	¼ cup toasted sliced almonds
New England clam chowder	whole kernel corn	1 medium tomato, sliced

1. In 1-quart casserole, stir together **Soup** and milk until well mixed. Stir in tuna, eggs and **Vegetable.**

2. Bake at 350°F. 25 minutes or until hot; stir.

3. Garnish with **Topper;** bake 5 minutes more. Makes 4 servings.

To Microwave: In 1-quart microwave-safe casserole, stir together **Soup** and milk. Stir in tuna, eggs and **Vegetable;** cover. Microwave on HIGH 8 to 10 minutes until hot, stirring occasionally. Garnish with **Topper.** Microwave on HIGH 1 to 3 minutes more until heated through.

Tip: *Toast almonds while the casserole is cooking in step 2. Simply spread almonds in a shallow baking pan and bake alongside the casserole 5 to 10 minutes until almonds are golden, stirring once or twice.*

Pasta with White Seafood Sauce

½ cup butter or margarine
½ cup salad or olive oil
4 cloves garlic, minced
1 can (10¾ ounces) condensed chicken broth
Herb
Seafood
12 ounces **Pasta,** cooked and drained
Grated Parmesan or Romano cheese

Herb	Seafood	Pasta
¼ cup chopped fresh parsley	1 can (6½ ounces) chopped clams	spaghetti
½ cup chopped fresh basil	1 can (6½ ounces) tuna packed in water	linguine
¼ cup chopped fresh chives	1 can (7 ounces) salmon	corkscrew macaroni
1 teaspoon oregano leaves, crushed	1 can (4½ ounces) shrimp, drained	medium noodles

1. In 3-quart saucepan over medium heat, in hot butter and oil, cook garlic until golden. Add broth and **Herb.** Heat to boiling; reduce heat to low. Simmer, uncovered, 10 minutes.

2. Add **Seafood** with its liquid (do not use shrimp liquid); simmer 2 minutes more, stirring gently to break up tuna or salmon. Serve sauce over hot cooked **Pasta.** Pass grated cheese. Makes 6 servings.

Tip: *It's easy to chop fresh herbs such as parsley, basil and chives with kitchen shears. For parsley and basil, place the leaves in a cup or on a cutting board and use the shears to cut them into small pieces. For chives, simply snip short lengths right off the plant.*

Souper Easy Quiche

4 eggs
1 can (10¾ to 11 ounces) condensed **Soup**
½ cup light cream
1 cup shredded **Cheese**
Meat
½ cup **Vegetable**
1 9-inch unbaked piecrust
Ground nutmeg

Soup	Cheese	Meat	Vegetable
Cheddar cheese	sharp Cheddar	½ cup diced cooked ham	drained, cooked chopped broccoli
cream of mushroom	American	6 slices bacon, cooked, drained and crumbled	drained, cooked cut asparagus
cream of onion	Monterey Jack	½ cup diced cooked chicken	sliced mushrooms
cream of celery	Swiss	½ cup diced cooked turkey	drained, cooked chopped spinach

1. In medium bowl, beat eggs until foamy. Gradually add **Soup** and cream, mixing well.

2. Sprinkle **Cheese, Meat** and **Vegetable** evenly over piecrust. Pour soup mixture over all. Sprinkle with nutmeg.

3. Bake at 350°F. 50 minutes or until center is set. Let stand 10 minutes before serving. Makes 6 servings.

Tip: *To make piecrust: In medium bowl, stir together 1 cup all-purpose flour and ½ teaspoon salt. With pastry blender, cut in ⅓ cup shortening until mixture resembles coarse crumbs. Add 2 to 3 tablespoons cold water, a tablespoon at a time, mixing lightly with fork until pastry holds together. Form into a ball. On lightly floured surface, roll dough to a 13-inch round. Transfer to 9-inch pie plate. Trim edge, leaving ½ inch pastry beyond edge of pie plate. Fold overhang under pastry; pinch a high edge. Flute edge.*

Easy Soufflé

1 can (10½ to 11 ounces) condensed **Soup**
1 cup shredded **Cheese**
Seasoning
6 eggs, separated

Soup	Cheese	Seasoning
Cheddar cheese	sharp Cheddar	dash cayenne pepper
cream of asparagus	Swiss	⅛ teaspoon ground nutmeg
tomato	American	¼ teaspoon marjoram leaves, crushed
cream of chicken	Jarlsberg	2 tablespoons chopped fresh parsley

1. In 1-quart saucepan, combine **Soup, Cheese** and **Seasoning.** Over low heat, heat until cheese melts, stirring occasionally. Remove from heat.

2. In large bowl with mixer at high speed, beat egg whites until stiff peaks form; set aside. In small bowl with mixer at high speed, beat egg yolks until thick and lemon-colored. Gradually stir in soup mixture; fold into egg whites.

3. Pour into ungreased 2-quart casserole or soufflé dish. Bake at 300°F. 1 hour or until soufflé is lightly browned. Serve immediately. Makes 6 servings.

Tip: *For best results when beating egg whites, bring them to room temperature before you begin beating. Be sure to use a very clean bowl and beaters; even a small amount of fat or yolk will inhibit the beating.*

Accompaniments

✤

Vegetables Oriental

1 can (10½ to 10¾ ounces) condensed **Soup**
2 tablespoons cornstarch
½ teaspoon sugar
¼ teaspoon ground ginger
2 tablespoons dry sherry
1 tablespoon soy sauce
4 cups fresh or frozen **Vegetable 1**
1 cup thinly sliced carrots
Vegetable 2
Garnish

Soup	Vegetable 1	Vegetable 2	Garnish
chicken broth	cut broccoli	2 cups fresh or frozen snow pea pods	diced tofu
French onion	cut asparagus	2 cups fresh bean sprouts	sliced almonds
beef broth	peas	1 can (8 ounces) sliced water chestnuts, drained	sesame seed

1. In 10-inch skillet, combine **Soup,** cornstarch, sugar, ginger, sherry and soy sauce. Over medium heat, heat to boiling, stirring constantly. Add **Vegetable 1** and carrots. Reduce heat to low. Cover; simmer 10 minutes or until vegetables are tender, stirring occasionally.

2. Stir in **Vegetable 2.** Cook until heated through, stirring often. Sprinkle with **Garnish.** Serve with additional soy sauce. Makes about 4 cups, 6 servings.

Tomato Vegetable Skillet

2 tablespoons salad oil
1 large onion, chopped
1 medium green pepper, cut into strips
1 clove garlic, minced
1 can (10½ to 11 ounces) condensed **Soup**
Vegetable
Seasoning
1 tablespoon lemon juice
Cheese

Soup	Vegetable	Seasoning	Cheese
tomato bisque	6 cups sliced zucchini	½ teaspoon basil leaves, crushed	¼ cup grated Parmesan
Spanish style vegetable	6 cups cubed eggplant	½ teaspoon oregano leaves, crushed	½ cup crumbled feta
tomato	4 cups fresh or frozen cut green beans	½ teaspoon thyme leaves, crushed	1 cup shredded Cheddar
tomato rice	4 cups fresh or frozen sliced okra	1 teaspoon chili powder	1 cup shredded Monterey Jack

1. In 10-inch skillet over medium heat, in hot oil, cook onion, green pepper and garlic until tender, stirring occasionally.

2. Stir in **Soup, Vegetable, Seasoning** and lemon juice. Heat to boiling. Reduce heat to low. Cover; simmer 5 to 15 minutes until vegetable is nearly tender, stirring occasionally. Uncover; simmer until sauce is desired consistency.

3. Sprinkle with **Cheese.** Cook 2 minutes more or until cheese is melted. Makes 6 servings.

Onion-Vegetable Bake

1 can (10¾ to 11 ounces) condensed **Soup**
½ cup **Liquid**
1 teaspoon soy sauce
Dash pepper
4 cups drained, cooked **Vegetable**
1 can (2.8 ounces) French-fried onions

Soup	Liquid	Vegetable
cream of mushroom	milk	cut green beans
cream of celery	light cream	sliced carrots
cream of chicken	plain yogurt	cut broccoli
Cheddar cheese	sour cream	Brussels sprouts

1. In 1½-quart casserole, combine **Soup, Liquid,** soy sauce and pepper. Stir in **Vegetable** and ½ of the onions.

2. Bake at 350°F. 25 minutes or until hot. Top with remaining onions. Bake 5 minutes more. Makes 6 servings.

To Microwave: In 2-quart microwave-safe casserole, combine **Soup, Liquid,** soy sauce and pepper. Stir in **Vegetable** and ½ of the onions; cover. Microwave on HIGH 4 to 7 minutes until hot, stirring once. Top with remaining onions.

Tip: *Buy 1 package (16 to 20 ounces) frozen vegetables, 2 packages (9 to 10 ounces each) frozen vegetables, 2 cans (about 16 ounces each) canned vegetables, or about 1½ pounds fresh vegetables for this recipe.*

Skillet Potatoes

3 tablespoons butter or margarine
1 cup **Vegetable 1**
½ cup **Vegetable 2**
2 cloves garlic, minced
1 can (10¾ ounces) condensed chicken broth
¼ cup water
4 cups cubed potatoes
1 cup carrots cut into julienne strips
Seasoning
Garnish

Vegetable 1	Vegetable 2	Seasoning	Garnish
sliced celery	chopped onion	⅛ teaspoon pepper	chopped fresh parsley
frozen French-style green beans, thawed	sliced green onions with tops	¼ teaspoon thyme leaves, crushed	chopped fresh chives
sliced mushrooms	chopped leeks	⅛ teaspoon dry mustard	toasted sesame seed
chopped tomatoes	chopped green pepper	⅛ teaspoon crushed red pepper	chopped pimento

1. In 10-inch skillet over medium heat, in hot butter, cook **Vegetable 1, Vegetable 2** and garlic until vegetables are tender, stirring occasionally.

2. Add broth, water, potatoes, carrots and **Seasoning** to skillet. Heat to boiling; reduce heat to low. Cover; simmer 15 minutes or until potatoes are tender.

3. Uncover; over medium heat, simmer 5 minutes or until broth is slightly thickened, stirring often. Sprinkle with **Garnish** before serving. Makes about 5 cups, 6 servings.

Tip: *You may be surprised to find that this tasty potato dish contains only 140 to 150 calories per serving.*

Broccoli and Noodles Parmesan

1 bunch broccoli (about 1½ pounds)
2 tablespoons butter or margarine
½ cup chopped onion
1 clove garlic, minced
1 can (10¾ to 11 ounces) condensed **Soup**
Seasoning
1 cup shredded **Cheese**
½ cup grated Parmesan cheese
1 cup **Dairy**
8 ounces (about 6 cups) noodles, cooked and drained

Soup	Seasoning	Cheese	Dairy
cream of mushroom	½ teaspoon tarragon leaves, crushed	American	sour cream
cream of onion	½ teaspoon basil leaves, crushed	Cheddar	plain yogurt
cream of chicken	½ teaspoon curry powder	Swiss	ricotta cheese
Cheddar cheese	¼ teaspoon cayenne pepper	Monterey Jack	creamed small curd cottage cheese

1. Cut broccoli into bite-sized pieces. In covered 4-quart saucepan over medium heat, in 1 inch boiling water, cook broccoli 6 minutes or until tender. Drain in colander.

2. In same saucepan over medium heat, in hot butter, cook onion and garlic until tender, stirring occasionally. Stir in **Soup** and **Seasoning;** mix well.

3. Add **Cheese** and Parmesan, stirring until melted. Stir in **Dairy,** broccoli and cooked noodles. Pour into 2-quart casserole. Cover; bake at 350°F. 30 minutes or until bubbly. Makes 8 servings.

To Microwave: Cut broccoli into bite-sized pieces. In 3-quart microwave-safe casserole, combine broccoli and ½ cup water; cover. Microwave on HIGH 6 to 8 minutes until almost tender. Let stand, covered, 2 to 3 minutes. Drain in colander. In same casserole, combine butter, onion and garlic; cover. Microwave on HIGH 2 to 2½ minutes until onion is tender. Stir in **Soup, Seasoning, Cheese** and Parmesan. Stir in **Dairy,** broccoli and cooked noodles; cover. Microwave on HIGH 8 to 10 minutes until heated through, stirring occasionally. Let stand, covered, 2 to 3 minutes.

Tip: To make clean-up easy, cook noodles first in 4-quart saucepan, then use it to cook broccoli, then sauce. Add broccoli to same colander with noodles to drain.

Macaroni and Cheese

1 can (10¾ to 11 ounces) condensed **Soup**
¾ cup **Liquid**
1 teaspoon prepared mustard
⅛ teaspoon pepper
6 ounces (about 1½ cups) elbow macaroni, cooked and drained
2 cups shredded **Cheese**
Topper

Soup	Liquid	Cheese	Topper
cream of mushroom	milk	Cheddar	1 cup French-fried onions
cream of onion	water	American	1 cup coarsely crushed potato chips
cream of celery	evaporated milk	Swiss	¼ cup buttered bread crumbs
Cheddar cheese	tomato juice	Monterey Jack	1 medium tomato, sliced

1. In 1½-quart casserole, stir together **Soup, Liquid,** mustard and pepper. Stir in macaroni and 1½ cups of the **Cheese.** Bake at 400°F. 25 minutes or until hot; stir.

2. Sprinkle with remaining ½ cup **Cheese** and **Topper;** bake 5 minutes more or until cheese melts. Makes 6 servings.

To Microwave: In 2-quart microwave-safe casserole, stir together **Soup, Liquid,** mustard, pepper, macaroni and 1½ cups of the **Cheese;** cover. Microwave on HIGH 7 to 10 minutes until hot, stirring occasionally. Sprinkle with remaining ½ cup **Cheese** and **Topper.** Microwave, uncovered, on HIGH 30 to 45 seconds until cheese melts.

Tip: *To make buttered crumbs, toss ¼ cup fine dry bread crumbs with 1 tablespoon butter or margarine, melted. You can buy dry crumbs in your supermarket, or make them at home. Bake bread slices at 300°F. about 20 minutes until very dry. Cool; crush with a rolling pin or in a blender.*

Savory Pilaf

2 tablespoons butter or margarine
1 cup **Vegetable**
½ cup sliced green onions
1 clove garlic, minced
1 cup **Grain**
1 can (10½ to 10¾ ounces) condensed **Soup**
¾ cup water
Seasoning
2 tablespoons chopped fresh parsley

Vegetable	Grain	Soup	Seasoning
shredded carrots	raw regular rice	chicken gumbo	¼ teaspoon marjoram leaves, crushed
chopped green or red pepper	raw brown rice	French onion	¼ teaspoon curry powder
chopped tomato	raw pearled barley	beef broth	¼ teaspoon oregano leaves, crushed
chopped celery	raw bulgur wheat	chicken broth	½ teaspoon rubbed sage

1. In 3-quart saucepan over medium heat, in hot butter, cook **Vegetable,** green onions and garlic until tender, stirring occasionally. Stir in **Grain;** cook 5 minutes more, stirring occasionally.

2. Stir in **Soup,** water and **Seasoning.** Heat to boiling. Reduce heat to low; cover. Simmer until grain is tender (about 25 minutes for regular rice, 50 minutes for brown rice, 1 hour for barley, 15 minutes for bulgur); stir occasionally. Add more water during cooking if mixture appears dry. Garnish with parsley. Makes about 3 cups, 4 servings.

Tip: *Regular rice is the rice grain with its outer layer (the bran) removed. Brown rice has most of its bran intact; that's why brown rice is chewier and takes longer to cook.*

Salads and Dressings

⚜

Garden Pasta Salad

¼ cup salad oil
1 cup sliced mushrooms
½ cup chopped onion
1 clove garlic, minced
1 cup **Vegetable 1**
Vegetable 2
1 teaspoon basil leaves, crushed
4 ounces **Macaroni,** cooked and drained
¼ cup sliced pitted ripe olives
1 can (10½ ounces) condensed Spanish style vegetable soup
¼ cup red wine vinegar
Cheese

Vegetable 1	Vegetable 2	Macaroni	Cheese
thinly sliced zucchini	1 cup broccoli cut into bite-sized pieces	corkscrews	1 cup cubed Muenster
fresh or frozen cut green beans	1 can (8 ounces) red kidney beans, drained	sea shells	1 cup cubed Provolone
fresh or frozen cut asparagus	1 cup diagonally sliced carrots	elbows	¼ cup crumbled blue cheese
fresh or frozen snow pea pods	1 cup cauliflower cut into bite-sized pieces	wagon wheels	⅓ cup grated Parmesan

1. In 10-inch skillet over medium heat, in hot oil, cook mushrooms, onion and garlic about 5 minutes until tender, stirring occasionally.

2. Stir in **Vegetable 1, Vegetable 2** and basil. Cover; cook 5 minutes or until vegetables are tender-crisp, stirring occasionally. Remove from heat.

3. In large bowl, toss together vegetable mixture, cooked **Macaroni,** olives, soup and vinegar. Cover; refrigerate until serving time, at least 4 hours. Just before serving, add **Cheese;** toss lightly. Makes about 5 cups, 6 servings.

Blue Ribbon Carrot Salad

2 pounds carrots, cut into 2 by ¼-inch sticks
1 can (10¾ ounces) condensed tomato soup
¼ cup sugar
½ cup vinegar
¼ cup salad oil
1 teaspoon **Seasoning**
1 teaspoon Worcestershire
Vegetable 1
Vegetable 2

Seasoning	Vegetable 1	Vegetable 2
prepared mustard	1 cup sliced celery	1 cup fresh snow pea pods, halved crosswise, cooked and drained
dry mustard	1 medium onion, sliced	1 green pepper, cut into strips
prepared horseradish	½ cup sliced radishes	1 cup drained, cooked cut green beans
chili powder	½ cup sliced green onions	1 medium cucumber, halved lengthwise and sliced

1. In 4-quart saucepan over medium heat, in 1 inch boiling water, cook carrots until tender. Drain; cool slightly.

2. In large bowl, combine soup, sugar, vinegar, oil, **Seasoning** and Worcestershire.

3. Add cooked carrots, **Vegetable 1** and **Vegetable 2;** toss to coat well. Cover; refrigerate until serving time, at least 4 hours. Makes about 6 cups, 8 servings.

To Microwave: In 2-quart microwave-safe casserole, combine carrots and ¼ cup water; cover. Microwave on HIGH 8 to 12 minutes until tender, stirring twice. Let stand, covered, 2 minutes. Drain; cool slightly. Proceed as in Steps 2 and 3.

Tip: *The dressing on this salad also makes a delicious marinade for broiled or grilled meats.*

Buffet Layered Salad

1 can (10¾ ounces) condensed **Soup**
1 cup **Base**
¼ cup grated Parmesan cheese
1 tablespoon grated onion
6 cups torn salad greens
2 medium **Vegetables,** thinly sliced
2 cups sliced mushrooms
2 medium tomatoes, diced
½ cup chopped green onions
Garnish

Soup	Base	Vegetables	Garnish
cream of mushroom	sour cream	carrots	sliced pitted ripe olives
cream of celery	plain yogurt	zucchini	chopped fresh parsley
cream of chicken	mayonnaise	cucumbers	chopped hard-cooked egg

1. For dressing, in medium bowl, combine **Soup, Base,** cheese and onion. Mix until smooth; set aside.

2. In clear 4-quart bowl, layer salad greens, **Vegetables,** mushrooms and tomatoes. Spoon dressing over salad, spreading to cover salad. Cover; refrigerate until serving time, at least 4 hours.

3. Sprinkle with green onions and **Garnish** before serving. Makes 12 servings.

Tip: *Use your favorite salad greens. Choose a mixture of iceberg, Boston, Bibb, romaine, butter, leaf and red-tipped lettuces, as well as spinach, endive, arugula, radicchio, watercress and parsley.*

Potato Salad

3 pounds potatoes
1 can (10¾ ounces) condensed **Soup**
¾ cup mayonnaise
2 tablespoons red wine vinegar
Seasoning
1 cup chopped celery
Vegetable 1
½ cup **Vegetable 2**
2 hard-cooked eggs, chopped

Soup	Seasoning	Vegetable 1	Vegetable 2
cream of celery	⅛ teaspoon pepper	¾ cup drained, cooked peas	sliced radishes
cream of chicken	¼ teaspoon dry mustard	¼ cup chopped green onions	chopped cucumber
cream of onion	½ teaspoon celery seed	½ cup drained, cooked diced carrot	chopped green pepper
cream of mushroom	⅛ teaspoon cayenne pepper	½ cup diced zucchini	sliced pitted ripe olives

1. In 4-quart saucepan, place potatoes; add water to cover. Over high heat, heat to boiling. Reduce heat to low; cover. Simmer 20 to 30 minutes until fork-tender; drain. Cool slightly. Peel potatoes; cut potatoes into ½-inch cubes.

2. In large bowl, mix together **Soup,** mayonnaise, vinegar and **Seasoning** until well blended.

3. Add potatoes, celery, **Vegetable 1, Vegetable 2** and eggs; toss gently to mix. Cover; refrigerate until serving time, at least 4 hours. Makes about 7 cups, 8 servings.

Tip: *Choose red potatoes or other round potato varieties for making potato salad. Or, cook small new potatoes for this salad, then halve them instead of cutting into cubes.*

Tomato French Dressing

1 can (10¾ ounces) condensed tomato soup
½ cup salad oil
¼ cup **Liquid**
Seasoning
Flavoring

Liquid	Seasoning	Flavoring
cider vinegar	½ teaspoon dry mustard	4 slices bacon, cooked, drained and crumbled
lemon juice	1 tablespoon grated onion	¼ cup crumbled blue cheese
wine vinegar	1 tablespoon finely chopped green onion	1 clove garlic, minced

In covered jar or shaker, combine all ingredients; shake well before using. Serve over mixed salad greens or fruit salads. Makes about 2 cups.

Creamy Salad Dressing

1 can (10¾ to 11 ounces) condensed **Soup**
½ cup mayonnaise
⅓ cup chopped fresh parsley
Liquid
Seasoning
Flavoring
⅛ teaspoon pepper

Soup	Liquid	Seasoning	Flavoring
cream of asparagus	¼ cup tarragon vinegar	3 green onions, thinly sliced	2 tablespoons finely chopped anchovies
cream of onion	1 tablespoon tomato paste	3 tablespoons sweet pickle relish	1 hard-cooked egg, chopped
cream of mushroom	3 to 4 tablespoons lemon juice	⅓ cup grated Parmesan cheese	2 cloves garlic, minced
Cheddar cheese	¼ cup buttermilk	2 slices bacon, cooked, drained and crumbled	1 tablespoon Worcestershire

In small bowl, combine **Soup** and mayonnaise; mix until smooth. Add remaining ingredients; mix well. Cover; refrigerate until serving time, at least 4 hours. Serve over mixed salad greens. Makes about 2 cups.

Sauces

❧

Sweet and Sour Sauce

⅓ cup **Sweetener**
2 tablespoons cornstarch
Spice
1 clove garlic, minced
1 can (10¾ ounces) condensed chicken broth
⅓ cup cider vinegar
1 to 2 teaspoons soy sauce
¼ cup **Vegetable**
Fruit

Sweetener	Spice	Vegetable	Fruit
sugar	¼ teaspoon ground nutmeg	sliced water chestnuts	1 can (8 ounces) mandarin orange segments, drained
honey	6 whole cloves	green onions cut into 1-inch pieces	1 cup pineapple chunks
apple jelly	1 stick cinnamon	zucchini cut into julienne strips	½ cup halved cherry tomatoes
packed brown sugar	⅛ teaspoon minced fresh ginger root	green pepper cut into julienne strips	1 can (8 ounces) apricot halves, drained and cut up

1. In 2-quart saucepan, combine **Sweetener,** cornstarch, **Spice** and garlic. Gradually stir in broth, vinegar and soy sauce. Over medium-high heat, heat to boiling, stirring constantly; boil 1 minute. Discard cloves or cinnamon stick.

2. Stir in **Vegetable** and **Fruit;** heat through. Serve over fish, poultry or meat. Makes about 2 cups.

Souper Gravy

Drippings from roast meat or poultry
1 can (10¾ ounces) condensed **Soup**
Liquid
Seasoning 1
Seasoning 2

Soup	Liquid	Seasoning 1	Seasoning 2
golden mushroom	¼ cup milk	¼ teaspoon tarragon leaves, crushed	1 tablespoon chopped fresh chives
cream of onion	¼ cup water	1 teaspoon Worcestershire	¼ teaspoon marjoram leaves, crushed
cream of chicken	¼ cup sour cream plus ⅓ cup water	½ teaspoon soy sauce	1 tablespoon chopped green onion
cream of celery	2 tablespoons dry sherry plus 2 tablespoons water	⅛ teaspoon ground nutmeg	½ cup cooked or canned sliced mushrooms

1. Remove roast from pan. Pour off pan drippings, reserving 2 tablespoons in pan.

2. Pour **Soup** into roasting pan; stir well to loosen brown bits. Blend in **Liquid**. Add **Seasoning 1** and **Seasoning 2**. Over medium heat, heat through, stirring often. Serve with meat or poultry. Makes about 1½ cups.

Tip: *If you do not have drippings, substitute 2 tablespoons butter or margarine. In 2-quart saucepan over medium heat, melt butter; stir in remaining ingredients. Heat through.*

Cream Sauce

1 can (10¾ ounces) condensed **Soup**
Liquid
Flavoring
Seasoning

Soup	Liquid	Flavoring	Seasoning
cream of celery	⅓ cup water plus 2 tablespoons dry sherry	½ cup shredded Swiss cheese	2 tablespoons grated Parmesan cheese
cream of onion	½ cup water	½ cup sour cream	⅛ teaspoon paprika
cream of mushroom	½ cup milk	½ cup cooked or canned sliced mushrooms	2 teaspoons chopped fresh chives
cream of chicken	½ cup light cream	2 tablespoons chopped fresh parsley	¼ teaspoon tarragon leaves, crushed

In 2-quart saucepan, combine all ingredients. Over medium heat, heat through, stirring frequently. Serve over vegetables. Makes about 1½ cups.

To Microwave: In 1-quart microwave-safe casserole, combine all ingredients; cover. Microwave on HIGH 5 to 7 minutes until hot, stirring occasionally.

Tip: *When you use a condensed cream soup to make a sauce, you don't need to worry about lumps because the flour is thoroughly cooked before you open the can. Any leftover sauce can be refrigerated and reheated later; thin it with a little water or milk if it becomes too thick.*

No-Cook Spicy Barbecue Sauce

1 can (10¾ ounces) condensed tomato soup
Liquid
2 tablespoons **Sweetener**
2 tablespoons Worcestershire
Seasoning
1 teaspoon dry mustard

Liquid	Sweetener	Seasoning
¼ cup cider vinegar	brown sugar	2 teaspoons chili powder
⅓ cup lemon juice	honey	½ teaspoon hot pepper sauce
⅓ cup lime juice	grape jam	2 teaspoons curry powder
¼ cup red wine vinegar	molasses	½ teaspoon ground ginger

In medium bowl, combine all ingredients; stir well. Use to baste chicken, spareribs, lamb, hamburgers or turkey. Makes about 1½ cups.

Curry Sauce

2 tablespoons butter or margarine
¼ cup chopped onion
2 teaspoons curry powder
1 can (10¾ ounces) condensed **Soup**
½ cup **Liquid**
½ cup **Fruit**
Garnish

Soup	Liquid	Fruit	Garnish
tomato	chicken broth	chopped tomato	raisins
cream of celery	apple juice	chopped apple	salted peanuts
cream of chicken	water	chopped pear	cashews
cream of mushroom	pineapple juice	drained crushed pineapple	toasted flaked coconut

1. In 2-quart saucepan over medium heat, in hot butter, cook onion and curry until onion is tender, stirring occasionally.

2. Stir in **Soup** and **Liquid** until well blended. Add **Fruit;** heat through, stirring occasionally. Top with **Garnish.** Serve over meat, poultry or rice. Makes about 2 cups.

Cheese Sauce

1 can (10¾ to 11 ounces) condensed **Soup**
Liquid
Cheese
Seasoning

Soup	Liquid	Cheese	Seasoning
cream of celery	⅓ cup milk	1½ cups shredded sharp Cheddar	½ teaspoon dry mustard
cream of mushroom	2 tablespoons sherry plus ⅓ cup milk	1 package (3 ounces) cream cheese, cubed	1 tablespoon Worcestershire
cream of onion	½ cup sour cream plus ⅓ cup milk	½ cup grated Parmesan	1 tablespoon chopped fresh parsley
Cheddar cheese	⅓ cup beer	1½ cups shredded Swiss	dash ground nutmeg

In 2-quart saucepan, combine all ingredients. Over medium heat, heat through, stirring frequently. Serve over vegetables, hamburgers or pasta. Makes about 2 cups.

To Microwave: In 1-quart microwave-safe casserole, combine all ingredients; stir to blend well. Cover. Microwave on HIGH 4 to 6 minutes until hot, stirring occasionally.

Tip: *This is a terrific sauce for serving over split baked potatoes. Make them into a main dish by topping with broccoli flowerets, chili, crumbled bacon or your own favorite additions before adding the cheese sauce.*

Carbonara Sauce

1 can (10¾ ounces) condensed **Soup**
Meat
Flavoring
½ cup half-and-half
Cheese

Soup	Meat	Flavoring	Cheese
cream of onion	6 slices bacon, cooked, drained and crumbled	¼ cup chopped parsley	2 tablespoons grated Romano
cream of celery	½ pound bulk pork sausage, cooked, drained and crumbled	2 tablespoons chopped green onions	2 tablespoons grated Parmesan
cream of shrimp	1 cup diced cooked ham	¼ cup chopped green pepper	¼ cup grated Gruyère
cream of mushroom	½ cup diced prosciutto	2 tablespoons chopped fresh basil leaves	½ cup shredded Swiss

1. In 2-quart saucepan over medium heat, heat **Soup, Meat, Flavoring** and half-and-half until hot, stirring frequently.

2. Stir in **Cheese** until melted. Serve over hot cooked pasta. Makes about 2 cups, 4 servings.

To Microwave: In 1-quart microwave-safe casserole, combine **Soup, Meat, Flavoring** and half-and-half; cover. Microwave on HIGH 4 to 6 minutes until hot, stirring once. Stir in **Cheese** until melted.

Tip: *Prosciutto is salted but not smoked, aged Italian ham that you can buy in your supermarket delicatessen. Have it sliced thinly, then cut it into small pieces for this recipe.*

Soup Surprises

No-Knead Onion Bread

Flour
2 tablespoons sugar
2 packages active dry yeast
1 can (10½ ounces) condensed French onion soup
¼ cup butter or margarine
1 egg
1 cup **Cheese**
1 tablespoon water
2 teaspoons **Topping**

Flour	Cheese	Topping
3 cups all-purpose	grated Romano	sesame seed
1 cup rye plus 2 cups all-purpose	shredded Cheddar	poppy seed
1½ cups whole wheat plus 1½ cups all-purpose	shredded American	minced dried onion

1. In large bowl, combine 1 cup of the **Flour,** sugar and yeast.

2. In small saucepan over medium heat, heat soup and butter until very warm (120° to 130°F.). Butter does not need to melt completely.

3. With mixer at low speed, gradually pour soup mixture into dry ingredients, mixing well. At medium speed, beat 3 minutes or until smooth. Add egg, **Cheese** and 1 cup of the **Flour;** beat 2 minutes more.

4. With spoon, stir in enough remaining **Flour** to make a stiff batter. Cover; let rise in warm place until doubled, about 1½ hours.

5. Grease 1½-quart casserole. Stir down batter. Turn into casserole. Cover; let rise until doubled, about 45 minutes. Preheat oven to 325°F.

6. Brush with water and sprinkle with **Topping.** Bake 50 minutes or until bread sounds hollow when tapped with finger. Remove from pan; cool on wire rack before slicing. Makes 1 loaf, 16 servings.

Tip: *When using a mixture of flours, stir flours together well before using. If you need any additional flour, use all-purpose.*

Cheese-Topped Sandwich Stacks

4 English muffins, split and toasted
8 slices bacon, halved, cooked and drained
1⅓ cups **Vegetable 1**
8 ounces **Meat**
Vegetable 2
1 can (10¾ to 11 ounces) condensed **Soup**
¼ cup milk
1½ cups shredded Cheddar cheese
1 tablespoon Worcestershire
½ teaspoon dry mustard

Vegetable 1	Meat	Vegetable 2	Soup
shredded lettuce	thinly sliced cooked ham	8 slices tomato	cream of mushroom
bean sprouts	thinly sliced cooked turkey	1 avocado, sliced	cream of chicken
alfalfa sprouts	thinly sliced roast beef	hot pickled peppers	Cheddar cheese

1. Place toasted English muffins on baking sheet. Top each half with bacon, **Vegetable 1, Meat** and **Vegetable 2.** Set aside.

2. In 2-quart saucepan, combine **Soup** and milk. Over medium heat, heat through, stirring occasionally. Add cheese, Worcestershire and dry mustard. Heat until cheese melts, stirring constantly. Pour sauce over each muffin.

3. Broil 4 inches from heat 1 to 2 minutes until tops start to brown. Makes 4 servings.

Tip: *For a lighter meal, just make the sauce in this recipe as described in step 2, then serve over toast or toasted English muffins as you would serve Welsh rarebit.*

Scrambled Eggs in Pita Pockets

4 pita bread rounds, halved
8 eggs
1 can (10¾ ounces) condensed **Soup**
1 cup **Vegetable**
Meat
2 tablespoons butter or margarine
1 cup shredded **Cheese**

Soup	Vegetable	Meat	Cheese
cream of mushroom	sliced mushrooms	6 slices bacon, diced	Cheddar
cream of celery	diced tomatoes	1 cup diced cooked ham plus 2 tablespoons salad oil	American
cream of chicken	chopped green pepper	¼ pound bulk pork sausage	Monterey Jack
cream of onion	diced zucchini	¼ pound pepperoni, diced	Muenster

1. Wrap pita bread in aluminum foil; bake at 350°F. 15 minutes or until warm.

2. Meanwhile, in bowl with whisk or rotary beater, beat eggs until foamy. Stir in **Soup** and **Vegetable;** set aside.

3. In 10-inch skillet over medium heat, cook bacon or pork sausage until done, or cook ham or pepperoni until heated through, stirring occasionally. Pour off fat.

4. Add butter to skillet; heat until foamy. Add egg mixture; cook until set but still slightly moist, stirring and lifting eggs so uncooked portion flows to bottom.

5. Stuff warm pita pockets with egg mixture. Add **Cheese** to each. Makes 8 servings.

Tip: *Buy pita bread rounds in the bakery or delicatessen section of your supermarket. They are usually available in white and whole wheat varieties. Cut them in half crosswise for stuffing.*

Sausage Breakfast Bake

12 ounces **Sausage**
2 tablespoons water
1 can (10¾ to 11 ounces) condensed **Soup**
2 eggs
¾ cup **Liquid**
2 tablespoons salad oil
1 cup all-purpose flour
1 cup cornmeal
¼ cup sugar
1 tablespoon baking powder
Butter or margarine
Topping

Sausage	Soup	Liquid	Topping
pork sausage links	cream of mushroom	apple juice	honey
smoked sausage links	Cheddar cheese	milk	maple syrup
Italian sausage in casings, cut into 2-inch lengths	cream of celery	chicken broth	fruit preserves

1. Preheat oven to 350°F. Grease 12 by 8-inch baking dish.

2. In covered 10-inch skillet over medium heat, cook **Sausage** in water 5 minutes. Uncover; cook until sausages are browned, turning occasionally. Drain on paper towels.

3. In small bowl, combine **Soup** and eggs; stir to mix well. Gradually stir in **Liquid** and oil; mix until smooth.

4. In medium bowl, combine flour, cornmeal, sugar and baking powder. Add soup mixture, stirring just to moisten. Pour into prepared baking dish. Arrange sausages on batter.

5. Bake 30 minutes or until bread springs back when lightly touched with finger. Serve warm with butter and **Topping.** Makes 6 servings.

Fruited Spice Cake Squares

1 package (2-layer size) spice cake mix
1 can (10¾ ounces) condensed tomato soup
½ cup water
2 eggs
1 cup **Fruit**
½ cup butter or margarine, softened
3 cups confectioners' sugar
1 teaspoon **Flavoring**
3 tablespoons **Liquid**
1 cup **Topping**

Fruit	Flavoring	Liquid	Topping
raisins	grated orange peel	orange juice	finely chopped walnuts
chopped dried apricots	vanilla extract	milk	granola
chopped prunes	grated lemon peel	apple juice	toasted flaked coconut

1. Preheat oven to 350°F. Grease 15 by 10-inch jelly-roll pan.

2. Mix cake mix, tomato soup, water and eggs, following directions on package. Fold in **Fruit**. Pour batter into prepared pan.

3. Bake 25 to 30 minutes until toothpick inserted in cake comes out clean. Cool completely in pan on wire rack.

4. In medium bowl, beat butter until creamy. Gradually add confectioners' sugar, **Flavoring** and **Liquid,** stirring until smooth. Spread on cake; sprinkle with **Topping.** Cut cake into squares. Makes 24 squares.

Tip: *This cake can be baked in two greased 9 by 5-inch loaf pans at 350°F. 45 minutes. Cool in pans 10 minutes, then cool completely on wire racks before frosting. Slice to serve.*

Spicy Vegetable Cake

2 cups all-purpose flour
1⅓ cups packed brown sugar
2 teaspoons baking powder
1 teaspoon baking soda
Ground **Spice**
1 can (10¾ ounces) condensed tomato soup
½ cup shortening
2 eggs
¼ cup **Syrup**
1 cup shredded **Vegetable**
½ cup **Addition**

Spice	Syrup	Vegetable	Addition
1 teaspoon allspice plus 1 teaspoon nutmeg plus 1 teaspoon cinnamon	molasses	carrots	raisins
1½ teaspoons ginger plus ½ teaspoon cloves plus ½ teaspoon cinnamon	honey	zucchini	flaked coconut
1 tablespoon pumpkin pie spice	maple-flavored syrup	peeled sweet potatoes	chopped nuts

1. Preheat oven to 350°F. Grease 10-inch tube pan.

2. In large bowl, combine flour, brown sugar, baking powder, baking soda and **Spice.** Add soup and shortening. With mixer at medium speed, beat 2 minutes, constantly scraping sides and bottom of bowl.

3. Add eggs and **Syrup;** beat 2 minutes more. Fold in **Vegetable** and **Addition.** Turn into prepared pan; bake about 1 hour until toothpick inserted in cake comes out clean. Cool in pan on rack 10 minutes. Remove from pan; cool completely. Serve plain or topped with whipped cream. Makes 16 servings.

Tip: *This cake can be baked in a greased and floured 13 by 9-inch baking pan at 350°F. 40 to 50 minutes. Or, bake in two greased and floured 9-inch round cake pans at 350°F. 30 to 35 minutes. Layer cooled cakes with whipped cream.*

Souper Cheesecake

1 cup **Crumbs**
¼ cup butter or margarine, melted
12 ounces cream cheese, softened
⅔ cup sugar
3 eggs
1 can (11 ounces) condensed Cheddar cheese soup
Flavoring 1
Flavoring 2
Topping

Crumbs	Flavoring 1	Flavoring 2	Topping
graham cracker	1 teaspoon grated lemon peel	2 tablespoons lemon juice	fresh strawberries
zwieback	2 teaspoons grated orange peel	2 tablespoons orange juice	fresh blueberries
gingersnap	1 teaspoon pumpkin pie spice	2 teaspoons vanilla extract	canned cherry pie filling
vanilla wafer	3 ounces semisweet chocolate, melted	2 tablespoons coffee liqueur	sweetened whipped cream

1. In small bowl, combine **Crumbs** and butter; mix well. Press crumb mixture into bottom of 9-inch springform pan to make an even layer. Set aside.

2. In large bowl with mixer at medium speed, beat cream cheese until smooth. Alternately add sugar and eggs, beating well after each addition. Beat in soup, **Flavoring 1** and **Flavoring 2** until blended. Pour over crust.

3. Bake at 350°F. 1 hour or until puffed around edges and set in center. Cool completely in pan on wire rack. Refrigerate until serving time, at least 4 hours. Garnish with **Topping.** Makes 12 servings.

Tip: *To make a cheese pie, prepare filling as above in step 2; pour into 9-inch unbaked piecrust. Bake at 350°F. 45 minutes or until set in center. Cool, chill and garnish as above.*

Index